PEARSON

LANGUAGE CENTRAL

ELD Song Book

Grade 3

PEARSON

Glenview, Illinois • Boston, Massachusetts • Chandler, Arizona • Upper Saddle River, New Jersey

Acknowledgments

Cover: Mark Buehner

Unit 1 Week 1 Maria Eugenia; Week 2 Christopher Lyles; Week 3 Hector Borlasca; Week 4 Red Hansen; Week 5 Michelle Gengaro

Unit 2 Week 1 Donald Wu; Week 2 Maria Eugenia; Week 3 Ethan Long; Week 4 Jill Dubin; Week 5 Dan Santat

Unit 3 Week 1 Barroux; Week 2 Jessica Secheret; Week 3 Laura Rader; Week 4 Sophie Casson; Week 5 Eldon Doty

Unit 4 Week 1 Matt Luxich; Week 2 Maranda Mayberry; Week 3 Jill Dubin; Week 4 Sue Williams; Week 5 Maria Eugenia

Unit 5 Week 1 Erica Pelton Vilnave; Week 2 Donald Wu; Week 3 Celine Malepart; Week 4 Red Hansen; Week 5 Jan Bryan Hunt

Unit 6 Week 1 Hector Borlasca; Week 2 Maria Eugenia; Week 3 Christopher Lyles; Week 4 Celine Malepart; Week 5 Ethan Long

ISBN-13: 978-0-328-65822-0
ISBN-10: 0-328-65822-7

1 2 3 4 5 6 7 8 9 10 12 11 10

PEARSON LANGUAGE CENTRAL

Table of Contents

Try Something New

Tune: "B-I-N-G-O"

Why always do the same old thing?
Today try something different!

CHORUS:
Try a thing that's new,
Try a thing that's new,
Try a thing that's new,
Today try something different!

Why not learn to bake a cake
Or how to **weave** a **basket!**

CHORUS

Maybe **camp** out in the woods,
Where there's a tent or **cabin!**

CHORUS

Read a book you've never read,
Or paint a pretty picture!

CHORUS

Trading, Trading

Tune: "Sailing, Sailing, Over the Bounding Main"

Trading, trading,
Trading is fun to do.
I'll give you some of my red paint,
If you'll give me your blue!
Trading, trading,
There's **plenty** that we can trade.
We both end up with what we want,
What a good deal we made!

Trading, trading,
Trading those for these.
I have **oranges** that I'll trade

For your **strawberries!**
Trading, trading,
There's plenty that we can trade.
We both end up with what we want,
What a good deal we made!

Reach Your Goal

Tune: "Here We Go 'Round the Mulberry Bush"

CHORUS:
If you have a **goal** to reach,
A goal to reach, a goal to **reach,**
If you have a goal to reach,
Work hard to **achieve** it!

It may just be that your **dreams** are
To be a **splendid skating** star.
On an **ice rink,** you'll go far,
If you work hard to achieve it!

CHORUS

If your goal is to be smart,
Here's a way to get your start:
Study hard, don't fall apart,
Work hard to achieve it!

CHORUS

Question of the Week How do we get what we want and need?

4

Wants and Needs

Grade 3, Unit 1, Week 4

ELD

Don't Give Up

Tune: "If You're Happy and You Know It"

If you ever face a problem, don't give up!
If you ever face a problem, don't give up!
When a problem faces you,
Do as much as you can do.
If you ever face a problem, don't give up!

If you're **stranded** on an **island,** you'll **survive!**
If you're stranded on an island, you'll survive!
Find the items you will need
Till you're **rescued** and you're freed,
If you're stranded on an island, you'll survive!

Find a hut or a cave where you can stay.
Find a hut or a cave where you can stay.
Yes, the hut or cave you're in
Will keep out the rain and wind,
Find a hut or a cave where you can stay.

Find some food you can eat every day,
Find some food you can eat every day,
Look around, and you'll see
There's a large **variety,**
Find some food you can eat every day.

Question of the Week What do we need to know about saving and spending?

5 Saving and Spending Grade 3, Unit 1, Week 5 ELD

Save Your Money

Tune: "Baa Baa, Black Sheep"

Save your **money,** that's a good plan,
Try to save as much as you can.
In the **bank,** let your money stay,
Your **account earns** more each day.
Save your money, and in the end
You will have more to spend!

BANK TELLER

Save your money, that is smart,
Now is the time for you to start.
Your account will grow in size,
You will see a **steady** rise.
Save your money, and in the end,
You will have more to spend!

Question of the Week What plant and animal structures help solve problems?

Animal Homes

Tune: "Home on the Range"

All creatures have homes
In the places they roam,
They **build structures**
So they can survive.
Some dig a deep hole,
Or a nest is their goal,
Their homes keep them safe and alive.

CHORUS:
Homes, homes all around,
Many animal homes can be found.
Each structure is strong,

So it lasts nice and long,
In a tree, in the grass, under ground.

A bird finds it best
To build a strong nest,
In a tree that is standing so tall.
The bird **pecks** and pecks,
As it builds, the bird checks
That the nest isn't **fragile** at all.

CHORUS

A Good Solution

Tune: "Do Your Ears Hang Low"

If you have got a problem,
Here's what to do, my friend:
Go find a good **solution**
To make your problem end.

A problem gives you **trouble,**
A problem gives you pain.
You'll find a good solution
If you just use your brain!

When you find a solution,
You'll know it's very good

If it ends the problem
Just like it should!

I **warned** you of the problem,
I told you what to do:
Go find a good solution,
Your problem will be through!

Question of the Week When is it time to find a solution?

8

Finding Solutions

Grade 3, Unit 2, Week 3

ELD

Time for a Solution

Tune: "The Eensy Weensy Spider"

When you face a problem,
Act right away.
Look for a solution,
Don't wait another day.
Tiny problems grow
To **enormous** ones, you see,
So the time for a solution
Is quickly as can be!

If you turn away
From a problem you've found,
The problem can spread

And get **scattered** all around.
The **path** you should take
Is very clear to see,
The time for a solution
Is quickly as can be!

Question of the Week What can we do to make sure solutions are fair?

9

Fair Solutions

Grade 3, Unit 2, Week 4

ELD

Be Fair

Tune: "The Ants Go Marching One by One"

To solve a problem as you should,
Be **fair,** be fair!
To find an answer that is good,
Be fair, be fair!
Be very **clever,** so when you're done,
All is fair for everyone,
Yes, when solving problems,
You really must be fair!

If there's a **treasure** to divide,
Be fair, be fair!

Don't give it all to just one side,
Be fair, be fair!
Do not act too **suddenly,**
Think about it carefully,
When it comes to answers,
You really must be fair!

Plants and Animals

Tune: "Jimmy Crack Corn"

A **desert** can get very hot.
Yet creatures live there—quite a lot!
Some plants live in the desert, too,
They somehow know just what to do.

CHORUS:
Plants and animals have learned to live,
Plants and animals have learned to live,
Plants and animals have learned to live,
They've all **adapted** well.

An ocean can be **harsh** and cold,
Yet creatures there are very old.
Some plants live in the ocean, too,
They somehow know just what to do.

CHORUS

Enjoy All the Beauty

Tune: "On Top of Old Smoky"

Enjoy all the **beauty**
There is all around,
The trees and the flowers
That cover the ground.

Enjoy all the beauty,
Wherever you go.
The new plants that **bloom** there,
The **bulbs** as they grow.

Enjoy all the beauty,
The **showers** that fall,

They help **create** new life
That grows big and small.

Enjoy all the beauty,
The **soil** in the ground.
Enjoy all the beauty,
So much is around!

Ancient Stories

Tune: "I've Been Working on the Railroad"

I've been reading **ancient** stories,
Tales from early days.
I've been reading ancient stories
That explain **mysterious** ways.
Some tell why we have an **earthquake,**
Or why a **rainbow** is in the sky.
People told these ancient stories
To explain the reasons why.

I've been reading ancient stories,
Tales from days of old.

I've been reading ancient stories
That explain what can't be **controlled.**
Some explain things **unpredictable,**
Like **dangerous** storms in the sky.
People made up ancient stories
To explain the reasons why.

Investigate Your World

Tune: "The Farmer in the Dell"

CHORUS:
Investigate your world,
Investigate your world.
So much is found all around.
Investigate your world.

Investigate the sky,
Investigate the sky.
Up in **space** it's quite a place.
Investigate the sky.

Investigate the stars,
Investigate the stars.

Millions glow with **gas,** you know.
Investigate the stars.

CHORUS

Help Animals in Danger

Tune: "Down by the Station"

We must **protect**
All animals in **danger,**
Those that are **injured**
Or stranded and in need.
If we protect
All animals in danger,
We will be helping the world,
Yes, indeed!

We must protect
All animals in danger.

Many **volunteers**
Can help those in need.
Finding **supplies**
For animals in danger
Is a way to help the world,
Yes, indeed!

The Things We Do

Tune: "When the Saints Go Marching In"

The things we do can change our world,
The things we do can change our world.
All that we do will have an **impact,**
The things we do can change our world.

We must **conserve** our water now,
We must conserve our water now.
Turn off a **faucet** when you don't need it,
We must conserve our water now.

We must keep lakes and rivers clean,
We must keep lakes and rivers clean.

Yes, it is **wrong** that we **polluted** them.
We must keep lakes and rivers clean.

This **simple** plan can change our world,
This simple plan can change our world.
Save all you can, and make things cleaner,
The things we do can change our world!

Question of the Week: How does it feel to be unique?

16

Feeling Unique

Grade 3, Unit 4, Week 1

ELD

Be Unique

Tune: "The Eensy Weensy Spider"

Do something special
And you will be **unique.**
People will talk of you
Week after week.
Being unique
Will make you feel great.
So do something special,
Hurry, do not wait!

Inventors are special,
They are all unique.
They push **themselves**

And work hard every week.
Being unique
Makes inventors feel good.
So make something special,
Yes, you really should!

Question of the Week What makes nature's record holders unique?

Special Places

Tune: "My Bonnie Lies Over the Mountain"

Do you know the world's tallest mountain?
Do you know the world's tallest **peak?**
The world's tallest **mount** holds a record,
A record that makes it unique.

CHORUS:
Record holders,
In **nature,** a place that's unique, unique.
Record holders,
In nature, a place that's unique.

Do you know the world's deepest ocean?
Do you know the world's deepest sea?
The world's deepest sea holds a record,
A record that makes it unique.

CHORUS

Question of the Week Why is it valuable to have unique interests?

18
Unique Interests
Grade 3, Unit 4, Week 3
ELD

Special Interests

Tune: "Yankee Doodle"

If you have a special interest
No one else has covered,
You'll become more **valuable**
For all that you've **discovered!**

CHORUS:
Your interests are unique,
Praise you will have earned,
Everyone will thank you for
The special things they've learned!

A **scientist** has an interest
Perhaps not yet covered.
A professor teaches different things
For students to discover!

CHORUS

Be the First

Tune: "Skip to My Lou"

CHORUS:
First, first, be the first,
First, first, be the first,
First, first, be the first,
Being first is a **privilege!**

Lead the group, so no one waits,
Be the first to open gates,
These are very special **traits,**
Being first is a privilege.

CHORUS

Set a goal, and then **campaign,**
Get elected, use your brain,
First-place **medals** you will gain!
Being first is a privilege.

CHORUS

Animal Behaviors

Tune: "Sing a Song of Sixpence"

Animal **behaviors**
Are special, that is true.
Animals can do things
That no one else can do.
A **porcupine** has **quills**
To keep enemies away.
Animals are all unique,
Each in its own way!

Animal behaviors
Are special, that is so.
Animals go places

No one else will go.
A bear sleeps in a cave
Where it will **hibernate.**
The animal kingdom is unique,
All animals are great!

Question of the Week How does culture influence the clothing we wear?

21 Clothing and Culture
Grade 3, Unit 5, Week 1
ELD

What We Wear

Tune: "Did You Ever See a Lassie?"

CHORUS:

Did you ever see how **culture**
Can **influence** our clothing?
Did you ever see how culture
Affects what we wear?

Some folks wear a **poncho.**
Do you wear a poncho?
Did you ever see how culture
Affects what we wear?

CHORUS

Some wear a **kimono.**
Do you wear a kimono?
Did you ever see how culture
Affects what we wear?

CHORUS

Some folks wear a **kilt.**
Do you wear a kilt?
Did you ever see how culture
Affects what we wear?

Different Cultures

Tune: "Goodnight, Ladies"

A different culture,
A different culture,
A different culture,
So many ways to live!

CHORUS:
Merrily we carry on,
Carry on, carry on.
Merrily we carry on
Traditions to remember.

Different clothing,
Different clothing,
Different clothing,
So many ways to dress!

CHORUS

Question of the Week Why is it hard to adapt to a new culture?

23
Adapting to a New Culture
Grade 3, Unit 5, Week 3
ELD

Hard to Adapt

Tune: "Oh, Dear, What Can the Matter Be?"

CHORUS:
Oh, dear, what can the matter be?
Coming to a new land are we,
But the changes are hard, you see,
Hard when you have to adapt.

To pack up your bags,
And leave your country,
To say a **farewell,**
And leave your country,
To part with your friends,

And leave your country
Is hard when you have to adapt.

CHORUS

You land at the **airport**
In your new country.
It's strange and it's **crowded**
In your new country.
You're **homesick** at first
In your new country.
It's hard when you have to adapt.

CHORUS

Different Foods

Tune: "Do You Know the Muffin Man?"

CHORUS:
Do you know the different foods,
The different foods, the different foods?
Do you know the different foods
That come from different lands?

Some eat **sushi,** a kind of fish,
Some like **pasta** on their dish,
For some a **taco** is their wish.
They come from different lands.

CHORUS

Different foods are often **bought,**
Different **ingredients** they've got,
Some foods cold, and some foods hot,
They come from different lands.

CHORUS

Question of the Week How does city life compare to life in the country?

City and Country Life

Tune: "Down by the Station"

Life in the city
Is very, very busy.
A **taxi** and a **subway**
Are in the **neighborhoods.**
Life in the city
Is very, very crowded.
Some city people feel that
An **urban** life is good.

Life in the country
Isn't very busy.

People live on farms
Or in a neighborhood.
Life in the country
Isn't very crowded.
Some country people feel that
A **rural** life is good.

Our Flag

Tune: "Polly Wolly Doodle All the Day"

Our flag waves high for all to see,
A **symbol** of the U.S.A.!
It stands for **freedom** and **liberty,**
A symbol of the U.S.A.!
Our flag's a thing we **celebrate,**
A symbol of the U.S.A.!
Our flag stands for a land that's great,
A symbol of the U.S.A.!

CHORUS:
Hip hooray! Hip hooray!
Let the **truth** be told this day!

Our flag waves high as we walk by,
A symbol of the U.S.A.!

The 13 **stripes** that everyone sees,
A symbol of the U.S.A.!
They **represent** the **colonies,**
A symbol of the U.S.A.!
The 50 stars we celebrate,
A symbol of the U.S.A.!
They represent our 50 states,
A symbol of the U.S.A.!

CHORUS

The Constitution

Tune: "Battle Hymn of the Republic"

The U.S. **Constitution** says
All **citizens** are free,
And everyone can **vote**
No matter what their race may be,
And everyone has equal **rights,**
Including you and me,
There's freedom for us all!

CHORUS:
How we love the Constitution!
How we need the Constitution!

It's because the Constitution
Gives freedom to us all!

The U.S. Constitution is
A **document** that's fair.
Amendments have been added
To the laws that first were there.
And each amendment shows how much
The people really care,
There's freedom for us all!

CHORUS

Question of the Week Why is freedom of expression important?

28
Freedom of Expression
Grade 3, Unit 6, Week 3
ELD

Speak Out!

Tune: "Hush, Little Baby, Don't Say a Word"

Speak, my friend, and say every word,
You have the right to speak and be heard.

Freedom of **expression** lets you speak out.
You're free to spread your ideas about.

You have the right for your words to be seen,
Print them in newspapers or **magazines.**

Share your **opinions** with folks you've met,
Put your opinions on the **Internet.**

Freedom **encourages** you to speak,
Don't be afraid, and don't be weak.

Speak, my friend, and say every word,
You have the right to speak and be heard!

We Need Rules

Tune: "Skip to My Lou"

CHORUS:

Rules, rules, we all need rules,
Rules, rules, we all need rules,
Rules, rules, we all need rules,
Rules are very **important.**

When you play in any game,
Being fair should be your aim.
Rules treat everyone the same,
Rules are very important.

CHORUS

Outdoors when two teams play ball,
Be truthful in every call,
Rules keep everything fair for all,
Rules are very important.

CHORUS

Just like sharing a favorite toy,
Rules are things we should **enjoy,**
Fair for every girl and boy,
Rules are very important.

CHORUS

The Underground Railroad

Tune: "Red River Valley"

Have you heard of the Underground Railroad?
It began in **the South** long ago.
It helped slaves travel **north** to gain freedom.
They kept it secret so no one would know.

Did you hear that the Underground Railroad
Wasn't really a railroad or track?
It was paths, secret roads, and safe houses
Used by slaves who said, "We're **brave!** We won't go back!"

They took risks on the Underground Railroad,
But there's always a risk when you flee.
Every stop brought them closer to freedom
And it's worth taking risks to be free.